Silke Vry

RED-YELLOW-BLUE

Colors in Art

CURR
N
7432.7
.V79
2011

Prestel

Munich • London • New York

LIBRARY
FRANKLIN PIERCE UNIVERSITY
RINDGE, NH 03461

CONTENTS

Follow these clues

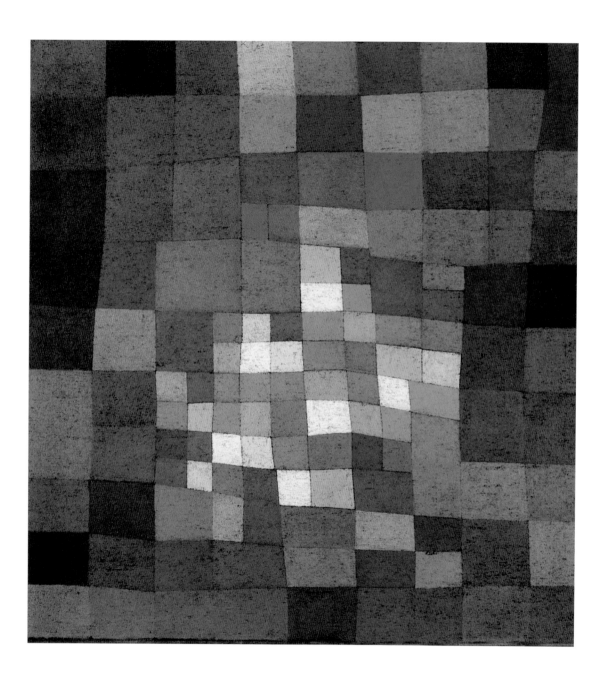

WELCOME TO THE GALLERY OF COLORS!

Angels are white and devils are black; love is red and taxicabs are yellow. We stop at a red light and wear black. Dragons are green and a "gray area" is not easily explained. A wedding dress is often white; and if you're feeling blue, you may want a pair of rose-colored glasses!

But why is this?
Why don't we imagine green angels or rose-colored dragons or devils? Why do so few brides wear black? And why aren't taxicabs usually gray?

If you want to understand color, you'll need to journey back in time – many centuries or just a few years – to meet the great masters and connoisseurs of color, and to see the pictures they made.

Would you like to come along?

BLACK AND WHITE

IN THE BEGINNING ...

... the Earth was totally "desolate" and empty, and it was also terribly, terribly dark. Many people long ago used to imagine the beginning of the world like this. Not particularly appealing, is it? And what color would you see if you could travel in a time machine back to the beginning of the Earth as early people imagined it? Actually, you would not see any color at all; only darkness darkness – which is the definition of black! No sun, no moon, and not a single star would appear in the sky. There would be nothing that could lighten up the darkness even a little bit. How dreary!

Black was also the worst punishment that a person could meet after death. **Hell was a black world** that consumed all light like a giant monster; a place without the smallest glimmer of hope. Could there be anything worse?

Where is black?

Everyone has two places on his or her body that seem completely black. They look this way because no light penetrates them. Sometimes they appear red, which is their real color; but usually you can't see them like this.

What are these places?

Read about them on page 86.

Do you know what it means when someone sees black, trades on the black market, is a black sheep, blacks out, uses black humor, gets blacklisted, or has a black cat cross his or her path? **This much is certain: it can mean nothing good!**

Read about it on page 86.

BLACK CATS – BLACK SHADOWS

People used to believe that evil spirits might be at work in the black shadows that followed people like living things. They ignored their shadows and banned the color black from their pictures – as far as this was possible. **Do you notice anything unusual when you look at this picture carefully?**

Read about it on page 86.

There's more to black than you think. An Experiment

You'll need a black felt-tip pen or marker, a glass of water, a knitting needle or something similar, and a clothespin.

Cut a strip of paper from page 89 and color the circle black. Then fill the glass with water, lay the knitting needle across the top of the glass, and use the clothespin to attach the strip of paper to the needle. The strip should hang from the needle and touch the water in the glass – but make sure the black circle does not touch the water. Watch what happens when the water begins to soak into the strip of paper.

Read about it on page 86.

COLORFUL BLACK

Black has always been a serious color: even today judges and undertakers wear black because of their somber professions. But black is not just the color of death and mourning; it can also express the beauty and energy of life. In the 1500s, European artists began to explore all the possibilities of black!

An artist who wanted to paint his subjects wearing black faced a great challenge: How could a picture have so much black in it and still be **radiant and energetic** – instead of somber or gloomy? If you look to the left, you can see that it's possible.

This painting by Dutch artist Frans Hals (ca. 1580-1666) contains no fewer than 27 different shades of black.

How many shades can you pick out?

WHAT DO YOU KNOW ABOUT WHITE?

What's the opposite of black? White, of course. If people used to think of black as the color of hell and evil, then they saw white as just the opposite: as the gleaming bright light of a better world. Even angels were given white robes as a sign of their heavenly origins.

In the 1800s, people greatly admired the **art of ancient Greece and Rome**. The ruins of ancient temples and the remains of antique sculptures were often made of white marble. So people thought that white was the color of antiquity: even the color of ancient clothing. But what they didn't know was that through the centuries the multicolored paint had flaked away from the temples and statues – and only the white marble remained. This misunderstanding led to a surprising consequence in the 1800s: **White became a fashionable color!**

Maybe you've heard someone say, "Black and white are not really colors." Seen purely in terms of physics, this is correct; for black is the absence of light and white is the opposite. But a painter would tell you something different: "Colors are what are in my tubes of paint." And of course black and white paint also come in tubes …

NOT BORING AT ALL …

When mixed together, black and white can create almost countless shades of gray. "Black and white" photographs use these shades to recreate the world around us in a recognizable way.

Black and white can also be used for a little **optical illusion:**

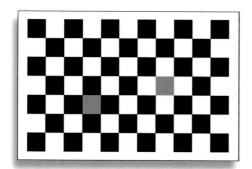
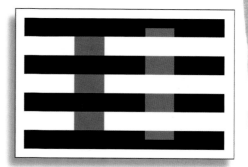

Each of these two illustrations contains black and white and two gray areas. Which of the two gray areas is the lightest?

Read about it on page 86.

In his painting Guernica,
Pablo Picasso (1881–1973)
painted **the horrors
and suffering of war.**
Picasso usually painted in
glowing colors, but he use
mostly gray for this artwo
What color could be bette
for horror?

GRAY OR GRUESOME?

As a color, gray was never very popular – and it still isn't today.
This is hardly surprising when one thinks of dismal gray days
and not-so-pretty gray matter! Because gray is a mixture of
black and white, it is a "colorless" color.
Yet for centuries artists used this color when they wanted to
paint something that really appeared gray; like a rocky cliff, a
cloudy sky, a mouse …

One of the first artists who dared to devote an entire picture to the color gray was the American painter James McNeill Whistler (1834–1903). He was able to breathe more life into a single color than almost any other artist. For this painting, Nocturne in Gray and Gold, Whistler painted almost the whole canvas gray. **He knew that gray could bring out the beauty in other colors.** And how! Don't the little lights actually look like they're glowing?

Gray makes other colors glow!

Try it yourself: Lay a little piece of colored paper on top of the gray square and an identical one on the white square. Look at the two pieces one after the other and see what effect the squares have on them.

RED

THE COLOR OF POWER

Long before freckled-faced, red-headed children began appearing in family photographs, there were people with bright red hair. When the ancient Germans went to war , they colored their hair bright red. They probably wanted to scare their enemies, for red hair was not something seen very often.

And when a Roman general returned home victorious after having bloodily conquered his enemies, he was allowed to paint his whole face red. Not surprisingly, he was cheered on by all who saw him!

Do you know why the fourth planet of our solar system is named after Mars, the red-clothed war god of the ancient Romans? Can you guess? That's right, it's because the planet appears red to us.

A long time ago it was possible to recognize powerful rulers by their beautiful and costly red-dyed clothing. But things have changed, and **today, anyone can wear red.** You can even dye your clothes red. It's easy ... Try it with a white t-shirt. To do so, you'll need the red juice from a jar of beets. Soak your t-shirt in the juice overnight, and on the next day rinse it thoroughly in the bathtub. You can fix the color by rinsing it in vinegar afterwards. Hang the shirt over your bathtub to dry. Just remember: never wash it together with light-colored clothing!

TYRIAN PURPLE: TRULY BEASTLY!

Imagine that you're walking your dog along the beach. Suddenly you discover something red on his nose. Is he bleeding? You wipe the spot with a handkerchief and discover that he's not hurt, but your cloth is now dyed a lovely shade of violet-red. The fluid had come from a snail that he bit into! And it's the most beautiful color you've ever seen …

Something similar was said to have happened thousands of years ago to the god Melqart. And the color he discovered in this way … royal purple!
Coloring clothes purple may have come easy to Melqart, but it has never been so easy for ordinary human beings …

Read about it on page 86.

Test your knowledge …

How many snails are needed to produce one gram of pure Tyrian purple dye?

a) 20   b) 500   c) 10,000

How long is it necessary to boil the substance from the purple snail to produce this dye?

a) 3-4 hours   b) 5 days   c) 2 weeks

How much would one have paid for a silk garment dyed entirely in Tyrian purple around 2,000 years ago (converted into today's prices)?

a) $ 1,700   b) $ 70,000   c) $ 1 million

And what does "Tyrian purple" look like? This is also not an easy question – on the color wheel, it lies halfway between yellow-red and blue-violet.

PURPLE PLAYS HARD TO GET!

When it was discovered, Tyrian purple was a rare, divine color; and for centuries it remained the color of royalty. Who else could have afforded the expensive purple clothing?

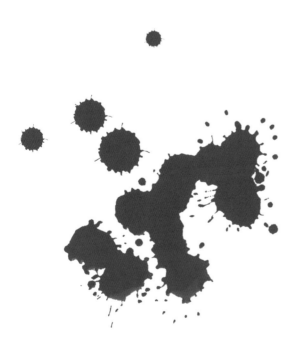

During their triumphal processions, ancient **Roman emperors wore togas dyed entirely of purple**. Later empresses and emperors followed this custom.

Look at this magnificent image of the Byzantine empress Theodora, a portrait that is nearly 1,500 years old! With her crown and purple robe, could there be anyone more beautiful?

IT ALL STARTED WITH RED

Even the earliest cave dwellers were completely enamored of red, the most
vibrant of all colors. Red was – and is – the color of blood. Red could be seen
whenever a person or animal was wounded. For them, like for many early
people, red came to mean life itself.

The very first images of people and animals in the Stone Age caves were
painted with blood. In this way the pictures came "alive" in the eyes and
minds of their beholders.

But when blood dries it loses its beautiful, brilliant color. You can see this transformation every time you cut or scrape yourself …

So when artists first decided to paint with a permanent red color, they chose red ochre – also known as the "blood of the earth." Artists from the Stone Age to the present day have used this color, and it remains very popular.

Cave painting for your room:

You can use tracing paper to copy these patterns below and transfer them onto regular paper. When you transfer them, enlarge the patterns and color them in with paint or markers – not with blood! Then crumple up the paper and stretch it out again. You'll have created pictures with a great "cave effect" that you can place on your walls.

GOOD OR EVIL?

Back when people still believed in devils and witches, they thought these beings must have had something to do with the "evil" color red. Devils always had red hair and eyes, and witches could be immediately recognized by their red hair – or so people used to think. Those were bad times for the color red!

Red, red hair ...

Would you like to surprise the people around you with red streaks in your hair? It's easy. You only need some red food coloring, hair gel, and disposable rubber gloves – which you should always wear when you color your hair.

Mix the color into the hair gel. Separate one lock of hair from the rest with a comb, place a piece of aluminum foil underneath the lock of hair, and brush the colored gel onto it. Repeat with other locks of hair. After about five minutes remove the aluminum foil so that the gel can dry.

Note: The next time you wash your hair (or get caught in the rain), the color will be gone.

Today almost everyone associates something nice with red: strawberries, raspberry candy, red roses, love ...

Red did not become the color of love just by chance; there's a good reason for it. Followers of Christianity came to believe that Heaven, where God lives, had to be red. The red color of Heaven symbolized **God's love**. So in this Christian painting, heavenly red angels float above baby Jesus – the son of God – and Jesus' earthly mother, the Virgin Mary.

How does red taste?
Try this game with your friends.
You will need to collect several edible red things: a piece of tomato, a red bell pepper, strawberries, chili (careful, not too hot!), radishes, cranberries, watermelon, red gummy bears, tomato paste ... even the leaves of (unsprayed) red roses. Now take turns tasting the foods with your eyes covered.
Can you recognize the different tastes?

Red can be dangerous! But is this true? Around 200 years ago, German poet Johann Wolfgang von Goethe (1749–1832) warned people against looking at red for too long. If you stare at this colored page for a few minutes, the red begins to "speak." But before you try to understand what it says, read Goethe's warning below:

"If one stares at an area that is completely red-orange in color, the color seems to bore into the eye. It produces an unbelievable vibration . . . even in a fair amount of darkness."

RED IS THE COLOR OF LOVE

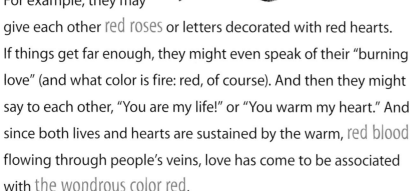

Not only do people in love occasionally have red faces, they also do strange things with red. For example, they may give each other red roses or letters decorated with red hearts. If things get far enough, they might even speak of their "burning love" (and what color is fire: red, of course). And then they might say to each other, "You are my life!" or "You warm my heart." And since both lives and hearts are sustained by the warm, red blood flowing through people's veins, love has come to be associated with the wondrous color red.

A declaration of love on paper:
You'll need scissors, glue, a sheet of red construction paper, two sheets of tissue paper in two different shades of red, and a photo of you and your best friend. Cut a heart out of the construction paper, cut a hole in the middle just big enough for the photo, and glue the photo behind the heart. Glue little crumpled pieces of tissue paper all over the heart.

The lady shown here is **Venus, the goddess of love**. Artists often depicted her stark naked. But today she can't go around everywhere like this! So you can help to get her a new, modern wardrobe. On page 91 you'll find patterns for clothing – but when you color them, remember that her **favorite color is red!**

Ever since artists have taken paint and brush in hand, they have thought about how their paintings will affect the viewers who look at them later.

HOT ON THE TRAIL OF COLORS

But at first, artists did not have a lot of freedom. In the Middle Ages, a period of time that lasted from about 1,500 to 600 years ago, European painters nearly always had to show figures from the Bible. And they were given very specific instructions for how a picture was supposed to look: the Virgin Mary should be dressed in red or in blue, no shadows please, not much green, and all the clothing and furniture should be of the best quality!

Now, as long as no one knew very much about colors and their secrets, everyone was happy. But then some people discovered their secrets and brought some light into the darkness ...

The English mathematician and physicist Isaac Newton (1642-1727) was one of the most important scientists of the modern age. His brilliant discoveries changed the way people saw the world. Newton investigated fundamental things. One of his main interests was explaining the origin of colors; not the colors in the paint box, but the colors of light.

For in order to understand color at all, you first have to know a couple of things about light. What do you know about it?

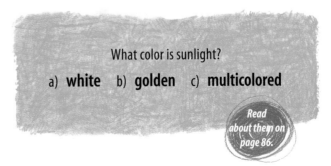

What color is sunlight?

a) **white**   b) **golden**   c) **multicolored**

Read about them on page 86.

"OPTICAL GHOSTS"

Newton discovered that sunlight is made up of colored light. This discovery was a sensation at the time. People had always believed that light could not be separated. In order to prove his theory, Newton held a prism – a triangular glass rod – in the white sunlight. The prism broke up, or "refracted," the light into various colors. Newton called what he saw a "spectrum," which is a Latin word for specter or ghost.

One spectrum conjured up by nature is the rainbow. Rainbows appear when the clouds recede and shafts of sunlight fall upon the drops of rain. The sunlight is composed of waves of colored light, and it is broken up by the raindrops – like by a prism – into its constituent colors. We see the rainbow as colored light!

You don't have to wait until the next rainbow to admire a spectrum.
Conjure up an apparition of your own.
You will need: a sheet of white paper, a glass of water, and sunlight.
Lay the paper on the ground near a window through which the sun is shining.
Place a glass of water on the windowsill so that it slightly (!) overlaps the edge.
The water now functions as a prism and produces a "spectrum" on the paper.

SHOW YOURSELF, BEAUTIFUL RAINBOW ...

How would you describe a rainbow to someone who has never seen color? How would you describe the blue of the sky or the green of trees?
Look at the girls in this picture: the older one is blind and cannot see the rainbows and sunlit fields that surround her. Maybe the younger girl can somehow explain these colorful wonders to her blind friend?

Read about them on page 86.

Do you know how many colors are in the rainbow?
a) 3   b) 7   c) 128

Newton's scientific discoveries also had important consequences for color in art. Now when painters thought of color, they no longer thought only of materials that came out of paint tubes. They also saw color in terms of light. Painters began to experiment with color: How does yellow react to purple; do red and green go together? They even came to realize that shadows do not always have to be black …

BLUE

A BLUE HORSE, HOW CAN THAT BE?

Looking at pictures by modern artists, you can discover a lot that's unusual, surprising, and dreamlike. You can see things that don't really exist: green faces, red fields, yellow cows, and even blue horses.

For hundreds of years, artists were most interested in reproducing what they saw with their own two eyes. German painter **Franz Marc** (1880-1916) wanted to depict the world in a completely different way. For him, the color blue had a very special meaning: **he saw blue as the color of dreams and of longing.** So he used this color to create his famous **blue horses.** When Marc founded an artists' group with his friend Wassily Kandinsky (1866-1944), they called it the **"Blue Rider."**

Franz Marc's blue horse is a very special creature; a being with a soul, dreams, and longings. And all of this because of the color blue!

How would your pets look if Franz Marc had painted them? How would he have depicted your hamster, canary, or dog? Try making a "portrait" of your pet using your own colors. How does it look: dreamy, snarling, fearful, or something else?

THE MOST PRECIOUS COLOR

The color blue has been precious for centuries ... precious and expensive! A long time ago, if you wanted to produce one of the most beautiful and lasting shades of blue, you first needed to buy a valuable semiprecious stone. You then had grind the stone down to blue powder – a laborious process! The color from this stone was of such incomparable beauty that people believed it had caught the light of heaven. They called it the "blue stone": "lapis lazuli."

The best quality lapis lazuli could be found only in northern Afghanistan, a remote region deep in central Asia. And since the stone had to be transported from there to Europe by sea, the color produced from it later came to be known as "ultramarine", which means "beyond the sea."

Until the 1800s, **ultramarine blue** was the second most expensive color of all; slightly less valuable than Tyrian purple. Ultramarine blue was even more costly than gold! Only the most important people and objects had the honor of being painted in ultramarine. One of the few people worthy of this color was **the Virgin Mary, the mother of Jesus**.

On the right, the Italian painter Raphael (1483-1520) depicted Mary surrounded by various shades of blue. **Not all blue shades were equally valuable** in Raphael's time, though they all look beautiful today. In fact, there is only one place in this picture where the unmistakable blue of ultramarine can be found. Can you see it?

Read about them on page 86.

Where can these colors be found in the picture above?

WHY IS THE SKY BLUE?

Everyone knows that the sky is blue. And almost everyone associates the color blue with the color of the sky. But how can that be, since air looks colorless when seen up close? The famous Italian artist Leonardo da Vinci (1452-1519) explained it in this way over 500 years ago:

> "I say that the blue we see in the atmosphere is not its real color, but is caused by warm water vapor evaporated in tiny atoms on which the sun's rays fall."

Only in 1871 did the English physicist John William Strutt realize that when white sunlight entered the atmosphere, it was broken down into individual colors. When the light shines upon the Earth during the day, only the short wavelengths of light reach our eyes. We see these as blue. When the sun sinks toward the horizon, it is the long red wavelengths that we perceive: the red evening sky.

Make your own sky blue

You can recreate the changing colors of the sky in an experiment.
To do so, you will need a glass of **water**, some **milk,** and a **flashlight**.
Stir a drop of milk into the glass of water. If you shine the flashlight
through the glass from the side, it will appear bluish. If you shine the
flashlight from behind, it will appear red.

Windows designed in blue can do you a world of good!

In the Middle Ages, glassmakers discovered how to produce **colored glass**. Unimagined opportunities soon opened up: it was now possible to make **pictures of light**. And these colors didn't just seem to glow, they really did so! The first colored windows were produced in the 1100s for the early Gothic cathedrals in France. They were placed in the cathedrals' huge windows, and their chief color was **the deep blue that represented both heaven and infinity**. When visitors stepped into these buildings, they were wrapped in a magical world of blue light …

THE POWER OF BLUE …

Have you ever finished brushing your teeth at night and suddenly felt wide awake? This might be due to the amount of blue light in your bathroom lamp. For some years now, we have known that there is a small place in the human eye that reacts to blue waves of light. If a lot of blue light reaches this place, then the brain receives the signal, "Wake up!" Modern scientists also agree that blue light can be good for your health and can free you from gloomy thoughts. Did the glassmakers 800 years ago possibly suspect this?

Would you like to paint a colorful picture for your window?

On page 93 you'll find a pattern and instructions.

COLD OR WARM?

Almost everyone associates blue with the color of the sky: distant, unreachable, and unreal. When we're cold, our lips turn blue; and in blue rooms our body temperature drops slightly. No, blue is not a color that warms you up. Blue is cold.

On the other hand, we see red in the mirror everyday: red lips, red cheeks. We turn red when we exert ourselves and when red blood flows to our faces. Red is the color of most blood, and flowing blood is warm!

Painters discovered the phenomenon of warm and cold colors hundreds of years ago. If a picture was supposed to show a cold place, then cold, cold blue would be used …

… Red also can depict things that are boiling hot. Look at this raging red fire!

Besides red, the colors yellow and orange can also seem warm to us, and so can brown and green. Besides blue, the colors violet and bluish-green can also feel pretty cold.

Many artists have understood our feelings about warm and cold colors, and they have used this knowledge to create exciting contrasts within a single painting. If you were one of the people strolling through this picture, where would you go to warm up on a cool evening?

NEAR AND FAR

With the help of warm and cold colors, it's possible to conjure up another "trick" on canvas. "Cold" colors — especially purple and blue — give the impression that they are much further away from us than "warm" tones like red, yellow, orange, or even brown.

During the 1400s, **Leonardo da Vinci** observed that as a landscape receded into the distance, it appeared to take on a bluish tone. He also had a good explanation for this discovery: there was so much air between our eyes and the distant object that it appeared to be blue, just like the sky did. Leonardo had just described the phenomenon of **"aerial perspective."** Do you see how incredibly far into the distance this painting seems to recede?

Painters who depicted nature in a more or less realistic way followed aerial perspective. They used cooler and cooler colors for parts of the landscape that were meant to be farther and farther away.

Living in the warmth of southern France, **Paul Cézanne** (1839–1906) painted many landscapes with aerial perspective. The houses, streets, and town squares in the foreground were shown in warm, sunlit orange and yellow; while the sky, sea, and mountains of the background were painted in cooler shades of blue and purple. These color changes are what our eyes are used to seeing in the real world.

But what would a picture like this look like if **the "temperatures" of the colors were changed around**: cool (blue and purple) towards the front, warm (yellow, orange, and red) towards the back? Try it: Color in the Cézanne picture on page 95 in this way and paste it underneath the "real" Cézanne. You'll be amazed ...

YELLOW

THE WARMTH OF YELLOW ...

Is there anything more sunny, warm, or radiant than a picture made up of shades of yellow? True, in freezing temperatures you can't really warm up your hands or light up a room with a yellow picture. But we still speak of yellow as being "warm" and "glowing." Why?

When we observe the natural world around us, yellow always seems to go together with warm, bright things. Look at the sun, for example. What color is the sun on a summer day? Since it's so bright, you can only look at it when it's lower in the sky, and then it appears rich yellow. But the sun doesn't just make everything radiate with light, it's also warm. It charms the flowers of early summer from the earth. Primroses, daffodils, marigolds . . . they're all yellow! So yellow is the color of summer, the sun, and the zest for life! What would summer be without yellow sunflowers and ice cold yellow lemonade?

Yellow is eye-catching!

It's no accident that taxi cabs and traffic warning signs are yellow! Whether you want it to or not, yellow catches your eye. Yellow can be perceived from the corner of your eye better than any other color.

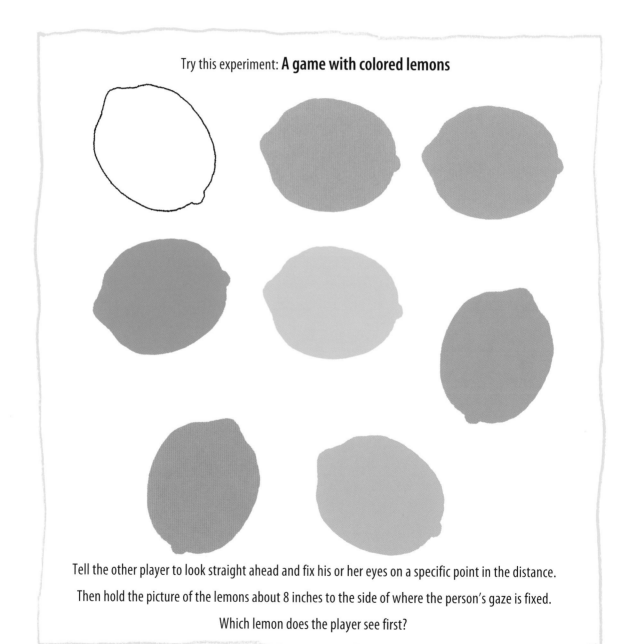

Try this experiment: **A game with colored lemons**

Tell the other player to look straight ahead and fix his or her eyes on a specific point in the distance.

Then hold the picture of the lemons about 8 inches to the side of where the person's gaze is fixed.

Which lemon does the player see first?

Thousands of years ago, Asian crocuses were used to produce saffron, the most expensive spice in the world! Saffron was also used as a dye for the most noble garments. Throughout Asia and Europe, yellow became a color of kings. And painters too loved saffron yellow on their canvases, a color that shone almost like gold …

But yellow is not always beautiful and sunny. Just one drop of black, and it is transformed into "dirty" or "shameful" yellow. Because yellow is such a conspicuous and radiant color, it was – and still is – used to draw your attention to something important or to warn against potential danger. A long time ago in Europe, many people who were considered "dangerous" were forced to wear yellow. They included executioners' wives, unmarried women with children, and people who practiced religions other than Christianity. Warning! When the plague raged in a city, the yellow flag was raised. It warned people to stay away from homes that were infected by this contagious disease. Yellow was also used to portray Judas, one of Jesus' disciples. Why? Jesus was killed, in part, because Judas betrayed him to his enemies.

For Franz Marc, whom you already know from page 29, yellow was a totally feminine color. He painted gentle and joyful cows, horses, and cats in radiant shades of yellow. Other painters, such as August Macke (1887-1914) and Vincent van Gogh (1853-1890), captured the atmosphere of warm places in shades of yellow.

Betrayers

Wealthy women

Yellow betrays the betrayer ...

Executioners' wives

Summer

...and much more

In the 1600s, a shade of yellow suddenly emerged with a radiant glow that delighted people. It was named "Indian yellow" after its land of origin: India. And it was not very easy to produce. If you'd like to know more about this unusual yellow, then solve this puzzle:

Below you can see nine details of pictures in this book. To solve the puzzle, you must recognize the objects shown in each picture. In the first picture you can see the sunflower from page 43. Write the word "SUNFLOWER" on a piece of scrap paper. The 2 in the first picture means that you will need to use the second letter of the word: a U. Write in the U as the first letter of the solution. Do the same thing with all the other picture details and letters.

Indian yellow is produced from the ___ ___ ___ ___ ___ of sick ___ ___ ___ ___ .

If you don't recognize one of the objects, you can look for it in the book.

Read about it on page 86.

WHO'S AFRAID OF
RED, YELLOW, AND BLUE?

Many centuries ago, painters found they could mix red, yellow, and blue to create all the other colors of the rainbow. Brilliant! Divine! These three magical colors must have come directly from heaven, people thought. The very first colors!

People called them "primary colors" (from the Latin word "primus": first). For this reason, painters made great efforts to achieve the finest shades of red, yellow, and blue. They also produced "secondary colors" by mixing two of the three primary colors together. Other colors could be made from the secondary colors.

In The Holy Family with a Lamb by Raphael, the Virgin Mary seems to glow in resplendent primary colors: **blood red, sky blue, and the golden-yellow of eternity.**

Primary colors cannot be made by mixing other colors. Red, yellow, and blue exist on their own!

Try it out: Which new colors are produced when the colors shown below are mixed together? It's best to use your box of watercolors. You'll see that all the colors in the world can be made out of red, yellow, and blue . . .
Can you also solve the last equation? (definitely not!)

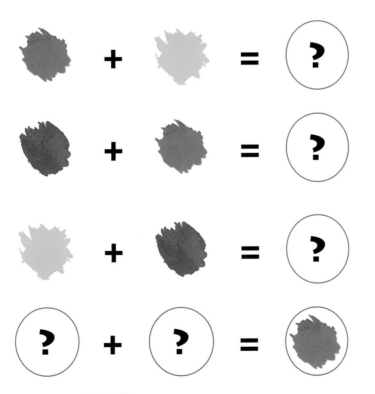

Read about it on page 87.

LIGHT-DARK CONTRAST

One painter who loved bright, glowing yellow more than just about anyone was Vincent van Gogh. He quickly used up his tubes of yellow paint, and whenever he ordered a new tube of yellow he always ordered a blue one as well. Can you guess why? No, not to mix them. He wanted to use them side by side on his canvas to make the yellow really glow. Below, you can see how he did this.

To the right you can see some of the stars from the painting below. Here, however, they're placed on a white background. They're pretty, aren't they? **But why don't they look like they're glowing?**

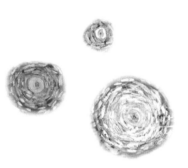

Now take a look at how a darker color can affect a lighter one: **against a dark background the lighter colors begin to really glow.**

Going bananas?

Read about it on page 87.

These three yellow bananas look pretty similar. **But are they really the same? Are they absolutely identical?** Isn't one banana's yellow color brighter and more glowing than the other two, and isn't it also a little smaller and thicker?

Yellow on yellow: Do you see how the lighter yellow steals the show from the darker yellow? The yellow banana is still visible. But with so much brilliant yellow around it, it doesn't really glow ...

Yellow on white: The yellow is starting to look a bit brighter. Not surprising, when its surroundings are so pale and subdued.

Yellow on black: Did someone turn the light on? The yellow here is not just bright, it's starting to glow!

Here's why: Our eyes always perceive surrounding colors, and we are strongly influenced by them. A colored background makes a similar color appear duller, a lighter background makes it look darker, and a darker background makes it appear brighter.

Many modern artists have used this "trick," which is also called "simultaneous contrast," to paint pictures in colors that seem to glow from deep within.

A Case in Point ...

Mixing colors is great. Blue and yellow will make green, yellow and red will make orange, and mixing all the colors together will eventually produce black. What more could any artist want? Yet mixing paints is not for everyone ...

One French painter caused a sensation with his extraordinary pictures. These paintings were **made from thousands of tiny dots**, each one of a single color. The artist arranged his colored "points" in precise ways on the canvas, one point next to another. When the viewer saw his paintings from a distance, the points would blend into the desired shades. The artist banned black and white from his pallet, instead using only the colors of the spectrum! But if you look at his painting on the right, you'll notice how he was still able to create the impression of black. Painters of these "point pictures" came to be known as **Pointillists**.

Play along!

On these pages are five details from the picture above. Can you find them in the big painting? If you line up the details – and their letters – in the order in which they can be found in the picture above (from left to right) . . .

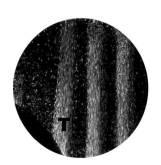

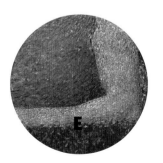

. . . then you'll discover the name of the artist.

Read about it on page 87.

GREEN

Green signifies life: If the green plants all die, then we humans will not be able to breathe any longer. This is why politicians in the "Green Party" are concerned about the health of our planet, and why they have long been telling us, "People, protect your environment!"

Read about it on page 87.

Get to work, green environmentalists!

Look at the image on the left-hand page. Polluters have thrown things into the green landscape that don't belong there. Can you find all ten things?

But it wasn't always so easy being green. To the contrary, there were times in the past when painters truly scorned the color green. Why was this? Because green is a "secondary" color, and it is produced only when the "superior" blue and yellow are mixed.

Look at how the painter of this picture depicted the **devil** many centuries ago: horribly ugly and green! **Green and evil** were soon inseparable, especially since the devil represented **poison and the stench of hell**. And of course it's no surprise that **dragons**, even today, are seen as not only dangerous and unpleasant, but also green!

And yet green is such an amazing color! Nearly everyone likes to take trips out in the countryside, especially in spring when the trees begin to turn light green after a long winter. And don't forget to bring some healthy green vegetables in your picnic basket! Or maybe you have a green thumb, and the gorgeous flowers in your garden make your friends and neighbors green with envy …

The singers of love songs in the Middle Ages, the so-called Minnesingers, cherished green as the **color of spring and the tender beginnings of love.**

Green is the color of life, of beginnings, and of hope.

Even hearts were originally green. The traditional shape of the heart, the **symbol of love**, is not based on the human heart but on the **green leaves of ivy**. Only later, after red became the color of love, did these "hearts" also change color.

GREEN IS FOR THINKERS!

Franz Marc, the painter of the blue horses, thought green was dull, boring, and stupid! And there is something about green that is different from the other colors. It lies exactly in the middle of the color spectrum, and this may be why it seems so balanced and secure. Green also improves concentration! Try it yourself:

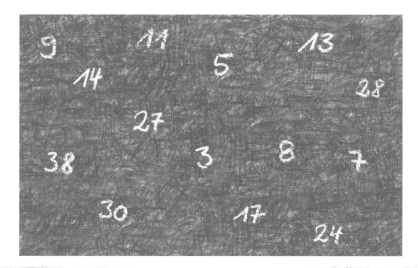

Look at the numbers on the green background for 30 seconds.
How many can you remember? Then do the same with the numbers on the red background.
Which was easier? Can you guess why so many "blackboards" in school are actually green?

SEEING GREEN?
ONE COLOR'S (SUCCESS) STORY

Step 1: Non-existent, but still visible!

For centuries green was avoided. But green doesn't let itself be banished as easily as that: you can cause it to appear with your own two eyes anytime. Even when it's not actually there!

Look at this red leaf for a whole minute in bright light. Then look at the white area next to it. Green appears!

Step 2: In the Middle Ages: the beginnings

Green emerges! Wherever red roses of love are in bud, green leaves cannot be missing. But you'll need a magnifying glass to see them!

Step 3: Green as the color of love ... between a man and woman. You can't miss it, especially when the green bride stands in front of a red bed. The colors compliment each other perfectly, just like the man and woman!

A small frog is hiding in one of these three pictures. Can you find him?

Read about it pn page 87.

Step 4: It can't get more green than this!

Paint tubes were invented in the 1800s, and they made it easier for artists to work outdoors – creating images of the green countryside. Green had finally become popular, even if people first laughed at seeing so much green vegetation in art!

GHOSTS PLAYING
"RING AROUND THE ROSY"

D

Mr. Newton was not content with his "apparitions" (see page 26). He continued searching and tried to figure out how the colors of the spectrum could be "arranged," and how they were already arranged in nature. Here too, he stumbled upon a brilliant discovery.

E

M

L

I

O

Maybe you've faced this problem yourself: you want to **organize the colored pencils in your pencil case**. Try it with these 12 pencils, which are similar to the colors of the rainbow. Start with the yellow shade labeled "M" and then try to find the pencil with the color that is closest to it. (When you do this, keep asking yourself, "Which color contains most of the previous color?" Remember, this task is not about arranging colors from light to dark.) Do this until all the colors and letters are arranged. Does your arrangement produce a meaningful word as an answer? Compare the last color of your row of pencils with the yellow of the first one. Do you notice anything?

Read about it pn page 87.

– – – – – – – – – – – –

U

L

O

C

T

R

Did you stumble upon the same discovery as Newton did when you tried to sort the pencils? Newton arranged the colors of the rainbow into a wheel. Brilliant! It had never occurred to anyone before that such a wheel was possible. Over time, other thinkers developed the color wheel further. Johann Wolfgang von Goethe added a new color (light purple), and Swiss painter Johannes Itten (1888-1967) gave the wheel a different shape.

The three **primary colors of red, yellow, and blue** form the center of Itten's color wheel. If you mix two of these colors together (yellow and red, for example), then you get a secondary color (orange). If you then mix the new color with yellow or with red, then you'll get the colors the lie between the **secondary colors** and connect all the colors into a wheel.

Try to paint this color wheel yourself with your watercolors.

OUR COMPLIMENTS, MR. NEWTON!

But before we give out more compliments of praise, we're going to examine another kind of complement: the complementary color. Among other things, "complementary" means "opposite." Each color has a complementary color, which is its exact opposite. But how can a color have an opposite? Complementary colors are those found on the opposite sides of the color wheel.

> If you were to mix two complementary colors of light, then you would end up with white! And when you mix two complementary colors of paint with each other, they will always produce brown. Strange, isn't it? You can find an experiment about this phenomenon on page 89.

Look at the blue star in bright light for one minute, and then look at the white area beside it. The color you now see is the complementary color of blue.

If you want to know a color's complementary color, you can either look on the color wheel, experiment with colored flashlights and watercolors, or – most simply – ask your eyes for help. Our eyes always try hard to see the complementary color. But what happens if a color meets its complement? Do you notice anything?
Of course: the two colors make each other gleam and flicker.

The same thing happens when an artist paints with complementary colors. In this picture, August Macke incorporated all the important complementary contrasts. This is surely why his colors seem to glow so strikingly!

In this picture, find the complementary color . . .

to the blue wall: _____

to the red fez hat: _____

to the purple roof: _____

Read about it on page 87.

CRAZY ABOUT COLOR!

After the invention of photography, artists no longer had to concern themselves with showing so many details in their pictures. Starting around 1850, many artists let the photographers do what they could accomplish better than any painter: to depict people and objects just as they actually looked.

Painters were now "free" to create forms and colors from their own imagination. The sky could now be orange, horses could be blue, and faces green.

Almost 300 years lie between these two pictures. Both show the same thing: a beautiful, young ... woman? But what a difference! On the right, delicate skin color; on the left, a bluish-green face. "Did the painters forget how to paint?" you may be tempted to ask when you compare the older picture with the more modern one:

Of course not. Do you remember the blue horse? Just like any other artist, the painter of the blue-green woman wanted to use colors to tell his viewers about the sitter. How did he portray her? She is shown as a thoughtful person who is, at the same time, strong and full of energy.

And now you can create your own pretty young woman. Be sure to choose your own colors and your very own style!

ORANGE

Quick, can you think right away of three things that are entirely orange (not including oranges, orange juice, orange sherbet, or the picture to the left)? Not so easy, is it?

Warm fiery red mixed with the radiant yellow of the hot sun: what do you get? Orange! Could there be a better color for pictures that show the heat and lushness of an island in the South Seas? French painter Paul Gauguin (1848–1903) found an exotic and brightly colored world on the remote Pacific island of Tahiti. He captured this world in his pictures, astonishing Western viewers. One color could be found in these pictures in abundance: orange in all its variations.

Many centuries ago, a new fruit called **"arangia" – orange –** arrived in Europe. This delicious fruit had an exotic color, one that Europeans had hardly ever seen before. The color didn't even have a proper name, so the people in Europe gave it one. Can you guess how they came up with that name? Well, what could be more obvious than giving the color the same name as the fruit? Brilliant or unimaginative?

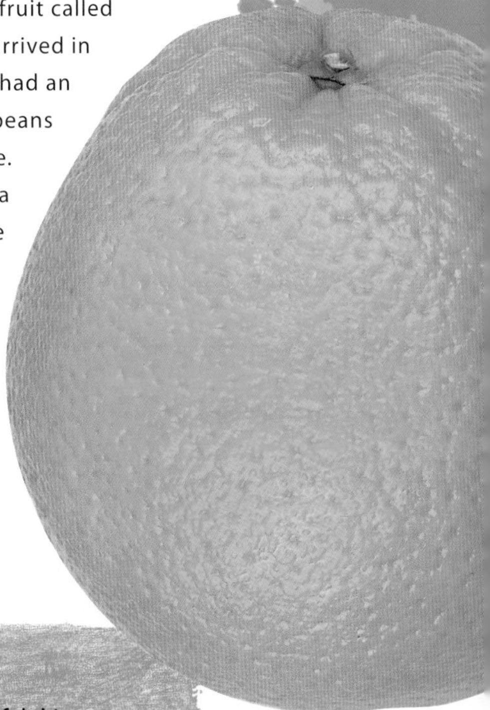

Round, orange, and mysterious

When the sun slowly sinks in the evening of a cloudless day, two wonderful things happen in the sky. The lower the ball of fire sinks, the more orange it becomes – and its surroundings become orange, too. But this isn't all. The closer the orange sun comes to the horizon, the larger it appears! People have always wondered about this strange phenomenon. Can you explain it?

Is it because

a) the longer wavelengths of orange light take up so much space in your eyes?

b) the sun becomes hotter and larger the more orange it gets?

c) your eyes are simply playing tricks on you?

Read about it on page 87.

65

If you look at a field of flowers in bloom on a sunny summer day, you'll discover many beautiful colors: yellow sunflowers, blue cornflowers, red poppies, white daisies, and of course green grass. But where is orange? In fact, orange appears quite seldom in nature. You can see it sometimes during the sunset, when only the longer wavelengths of light penetrate the atmosphere and create an orange sky.

Make your own orange flower. You'll need a freshly-cut white flower (carnation, rose, . . .), one tube each of red and yellow food coloring, and a glass of water. Add a few drops of both the yellow and red food coloring to the water and stir them in. Then place the flower in the glass and wait for a while. Eventually the colored water will begin to be absorbed, coloring the white flower petals orange.

DID YOU KNOW?

Orange is exciting: Spending time in a room painted entirely orange will stimulate your circulation; which means that blood flows more quickly through your veins. And the color can warm you up, too. In an orange room, people start to feel cold only when the temperature falls to 52 degrees Fahrenheit (in comparison, a blue room already starts to feel uncomfortably cold at 59 degrees).

Why does the Dalai Lama wear orange? He is one of the leading figures of Buddhism, a major religion in southern and eastern Asia. Orange has been known in Buddhist countries for thousands of years, and it is considered the color of enlightenment – the highest state of being that Buddhists can achieve. Orange is also known as the the color of fire and wisdom.

Whenever night falls,
it is accompanied by a great, mysterious monster that robs all things of their color and throws them into a deep, black hole. Now does this really sound true? I wouldn't believe it!

WHAT HAPPENS TO COLORS AT NIGHT?

Look at the leaves of a tree in bright sunlight. What do you see? You'll notice that they're green, of course (if it doesn't happen to be autumn). If you look at the same leaves in the dark, however, you will see that they're no longer green, but black. This is why:

Sunlight is so bright that it might even seem to be white. But Mr. Newton and some of his colleagues have shown that white sunlight is actually composed of many different colors (for this reason physicists do not consider white and black to be true colors; since white contains all the colors of sunlight, and black, in contrast, is the absence of all color). The leaves of the tree that we see on a summer day only appear green. This is because they reflect back the green wavelengths of sunlight and absorb the other ones. At night the leaves appear black, since no light is available to be reflected back as colors. This is how the "black of night" comes about.

A green leaf, an orange, a lemon, etc., will appear to be their usual colors only when you look at them in white light. **But if you change the color of the light, you will notice something amazing:**

Cut a large hole in the lid of a shoebox and cover it with green **tracing paper**. Then cut a small peephole in the side wall of the **shoebox**. Place an object – a **tomato**, a green **apple**, or a **banana**, for example – in the box and close the lid. Take the box into a dark room, shine a **flashlight** onto the object through the colored lid, and watch what happens through the peephole. The banana takes on a greenish hue, the tomato looks black …

Why

The green paper allows only the green light of the flashlight through. Since green light contains no red, the tomato can't reflect back any red light!

VIOLET

A LOT OF RED, A LOT OF BLUE: VIOLET!

The name for the color violet comes, not surprisingly, from the flower "violet." People have long cherished this pretty, sweet-smelling flower. And because violets grow low upon the ground, people have associated the flowers with the admirable human virtue of humility. Painters sometimes showed the Virgin Mary picking violets or holding them in her hands. Eventually, the color of the violet became just as special as the flower itself. It came to represent modesty and mourning.

For no good reason, the violet flowers that gave their name to the color have been forgotten by many people today. But surely it's not only grand-mothers who are delighted by the flowers' scent or by old-fashioned candied violets …

Magical, changeable violet

Red cabbage is a color just between red and blue. Since there wasn't yet any name for this color in the Middle Ages, the cabbage came to be called "red." The violet juice of the plant's leaves can be used in colorful experiments. Try this one: chop up some fresh leaves of red cabbage, put them in a pot with some water, and boil them for a few minutes until the water has turned violet. Let the mixture cool down and then pour it through a sieve. Now the magic liquid is ready to use. Try putting just a couple of drops of the juice in various other liquids (mineral water, lemonade, vinegar, soapy water) and watch how violet transforms itself!

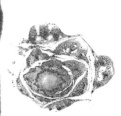

PINK

Love is a cake with pink frosting...! Roses are often pink, and the word rose is used to mean pink. To lovers, the whole world seems rosy. And whoever sees only the dark side of things needs a pair of rose-colored glasses!

Pink can make your spirits soar! The young lady in pink has kicked off one of her rosy shoes while swinging – something that would never have happened with shoes of any other color! Can you help her find it?

Read about it on page 87.

Have you ever looked through rose-colored glasses?
If not, then it's about time!

Make your own pair of rose-colored glasses:
You'll find a pattern and instructions on page 89.

As soon as you look through these glasses, you'll notice that everything suddenly looks like part of a beautiful fairy tale. Worries and problems? There don't seem to be any such things in a rose-colored world!

Tell me your name, please ...
and I'll tell you what color you are!
Is your name in one of the lists below?

Amber
(English: "golden-yellow")
  Aurora
  (Latin: dawn)
    Bianca
    (Italian: white)
    Carmine
    (Latin: vivid red)
    Gwendolyn
    (English/Celtic: "gwen" = white)
    Melanie
    (Greek: "mélas" = black)
    Rosa
    (Italian: rose-colored)
    Ruth
    (Hebrew: "the red one")

Scarlett
(Old French: red)
  Violet
  (Latin: purple)

    Bruno (old German name
    meaning "the brown one")
    Brunold
    (the "brown one" and "to rule")
    Candide
    (Latin: radiant white")
    Chrysostom
    (Greek: "golden mouth")
    Douglas
    (English/Celtic: dark blue)
    Flavio (Latin: "the blond one")
    Rufus (Latin: "the red one")

Girls' names can be just as red, blonde, or golden as those of boys. But do you notice an important difference between the girls' names and the boys' names? That's right, it's only the girls whose names are sometimes pink or violet.
In fact it's still very common today for parents to dress their newborn daughters in pink. And no one who looks at a baby dressed in pink would think to ask,

"Is it a boy or a girl?"

So do you think pink is a typical girls' color?

Long ago this attitude was very different. Whenever someone saw a baby wrapped in pink, they knew right away that "This must be a boy, of course!" In the past, red was the color of rulers; and rulers were mostly men.
But for these men's sons, a "small" red was reserved: pink.
This is why Claude Monet painted his son in a pink dress.
Blue, on the other hand, was the color of Mary in the Bible; and because of her, blue became a feminine color. Wealthy parents had magnificent dresses of precious blue fabric made for their daughters. In fact, it was not unusual to see many little girls dressed in light blue. This state of affairs first changed around 80 years ago, as sailors and workers began to wear blue in the form of blue coveralls or, more famously, blue jeans. Only then did the "small" blue – light blue – begin to be associated with little boys.

LISTEN TO THE BEAUTIFUL COLORS!

Many centuries ago, people began to notice that colors and notes had a lot in common. Just as notes had to be "in tune with" one another in a musical composition, so colors had to match one another in a painting. Musical composers could make each note a little higher or lower. Painters could make each shade of color a little lighter or deeper. And both notes and areas of color had to be arranged in the right "rhythm" to create pleasing musical and visual "compositions."

In painting we speak of "tone," and in music we speak of "tone color" or timber ... and a composition can be made up of notes or of colors.

Does a flute sound blue to your ear? A trumpet red? Then maybe you can hear colors? ... This rare gift is called synesthesia. Modern scientists who study these things believe that many babies and children can still see music in color. Sadly, most lose this ability later in life.

If you'd like to find out if someone can see color in music, then try this experiment.

You'll need some music, a CD player, paper, colored pencils or crayons, and a stopwatch. Play a song that is not too fast for your test subject. Measure the time from the beginning of the piece of music to the point at which your subject completes his or her first, second, or third drawing.

Repeat the same experiment a few days later. Does your subject create similar drawings each time? If he or she does, then you may have discovered someone with a very special talent!

The Russian painter Wassily Kandinsky could truly hear in color. In some of his paintings, he translated the vibrations of specific musical pieces into colored compositions. **Do you hear anything** in the painting shown above?

BROWN

Did you know that brown was long considered the ugliest color imaginable? The main reason for this attitude: brown is not a primary color. It is only produced when several other colors are mixed together. You can't even find brown in the rainbow!

For many centuries, **brown was the color of people who were poor or invisible: peasants and servants, beggars and monks.** These individuals wore brownish, undyed clothing; and they all looked a bit scruffy and unsophisticated.

Of course, people had always needed brown. But they refused to grind down precious stones to get it. Unthinkable! Brown color was obtained from anything people happened to find: ochre clay from the earth, sepia from the brown "ink" of a squid's inc sac, or even the ground-up bodies of ancient Egyptian mummies ("mummy powder")!

Only over the course of many centuries did brown – the color of forgotten people – turn into **the color of coziness.** You can see this change in the picture to the left by German artist Adolf von Menzel (1815–1905). Menzel felt that the evenings with his mother and sister were warm and comforting, and he painted them brown …

Warm and comforting? That sounds like **homemade chocolate fondue!** To make it you'll need one bar of bittersweet chocolate, a bar of milk chocolate, a ¾ cup of heavy cream, squares of white bread or sponge cake, various kinds of fruit cut into pieces, shish-kebab skewers, and a tea warmer. Break the chocolate into pieces and slowly melt it over low heat. Then add the heavy cream. Transfer the fondue into a fondue pot, but be careful to heat it only with the tea warmer. Now you can dip the fruit into the liquid chocolate. Enjoy!

GOLD

There is no such color as "gold," – it appears nowhere in the color spectrum.
Yet the precious, yellowish metal called gold has long been prized for its sparkle.

People long ago believed that they could see the light of heaven in gold and its shine.

For the ancient Egyptians, anyone whose image was fashioned in gold was guaranteed a heavenly, immortal afterlife. For thousands of years, gold has been the metal of kings, priests, and gods – all the rulers of this world and the one beyond.

How would you like to wear a golden mask next Halloween; one that makes you **look like a king from ancient, mythical times?** You'll need a sheet of thin but sturdy gold foil from the craft store. Instructions can be found on page 95.

Here are two pictures of the same lady on a gold background. But which one is the "real" lady? A forger has been at work here and tried to copy the famous painting. But he made seven mistakes. Can you find them? Which is the "forgery" and which is the "original"?

Read about it on page 87.

NOT EVERYTHING THAT GLITTERS IS GOLD.

Look at these six details from famous artworks. On four of them, gold-like color was painted on the canvas to look like real, shimmering gold metal. The artists created this fake gold by mixing yellow, ochre, and white paint. On the other two artworks, however, the "gold" is real. Can you find the real gold?

Read about it on page 87.

The Works of Art in this Book

Answers

Page 7
Where is black?

The blackest places on your body are your two pupils, which are nothing but circular holes in your eyes. Each exists inside the colorful part of the eye called the iris. Behind each of these openings is the retina, which is well supplied with blood. When you look into the flash of a camera, you later appear in the photograph with glaring red eyes. Why? Because the bright light reaches the blood-red retina, which is otherwise almost always in the dark.

Page 8
Someone who …

sees black doesn't always perceive the good in life; someone who trades on the black market sells things illegally; a black sheep is not accepted by others; someone who has blacked out has lost consciousness; someone with black humor treats serious topics in a slightly funny way; someone who has been blacklisted is not allowed to work or participate in certain activities; and if a black cat crosses your path, you might suffer bad luck.

Black shadows …

Actually, this artist did try hard to paint his individual people, plants, and buildings realistically. But we should expect to see shadows next to the people and trees … something the painter has left out. So the figures look almost like they're floating. There may be lighter and darker areas in the robes, in the treetops, and on the tree trunks – but there are no real shadows. Perhaps the artist did this because of his belief in the Bible's description of God and the Creation. God was seen as the "light of the world," and people, animals, and plants were seen as creatures of God. No dark shadows should mar God's creations!

There's more than you think to black!

When the strip of paper becomes soaked with water, the black circle made by the felt-tip pen or marker reveals many other colors – the colors that make up black. You can also try this experiment with other colored markers, and find out what colors the various markers contain.

Page 11
Optical Illusion

The two gray squares are completely identical in color, and so are the two gray beams!
How is this possible? We perceive differences in lightness very "subjectively," by comparing each shade with its surroundings and then deciding, "This shade is lighter!" or "this shade is darker!" A shade of color may appear light to us when seen in a dark environment, but that same shade can look dark when seen in bright light.

Page 16
Test your knowledge of Tyrian purple.

The correct answers are 1 c), 2 c), and 3 b).

Page 25
The color of sunlight …

Answer c) is correct.

Page 27
How many colors are in the rainbow …

Answer b) is correct

Page 30-1
Where is the precious blue?

The precious ultramarine blue is hidden in Mary's robe (detail no. 3).

Page 45:
Indian yellow

The answer is: From the urine of sick cows.

1. SUNFLOWER
2. SAFFRON
3. VIOLET
4. MOON
5. COW
6. BRIDGE
7. CHAIR
8. HORSE
9. DOG

To obtain the incomparably brilliant hue of Indian yellow, the cows were given special leaves that did not agree with them and colored their urine a deep yellow. The urine was dried and made into little balls that were then sold as paint, especially for watercolors. In 1921, the sale of true Indian Yellow was forbidden.

Page 47
Who's Afraid of Red, Yellow, and Blue?
Red + yellow = orange
Blue + red = violet
Yellow + blue = green
The last equation cannot be solved, since red cannot be mixed from other colors.

Page 49
Going bananas?
The three bananas are completely the same.
If they look different to you, your eyes are playing tricks on you.

Page 50-1
Case in Point ...
The painter's name is: Georges SEURAT. He lived from 1859 to 1891 and was the founder of painting with points, or "Pointillism."

Page 54-5
Green environmentalists, to work!
The trash is circled in red.

Page 56-7
Where is the frog?
The frog is hiding on the young bride's green coat on page 57.

Page 58
Ghosts Playing "Ring around the Rosie"
If you arranged the 12 colored pencils so that their letters spell out the word "multicolored," then you arranged them just as Mr. Newton did. Congratulations! The first (yellow) and the last (green) are similar in shade. If you wanted to, you could turn the row into a circle!

Page 61
August Macke
The pairs of complementary colors are:
Blue wall, orange door
Red fez, green leaves
Violet roof, yellow chair

Page 65
Orange, round, and mysterious
Answer no. 3 is correct.

Page 72
Pink can make your spirits soar!
The young lady's shoe has flown all the way to the tree trunk at the lower right.

Page 82
Original and Forgery
The real painting is the one on the right. The forgery is on the left, with red circles around the mistakes.

Page 83
Not everything that glitters is gold
The real gold can be found in the left-hand picture in the top row and the right-hand picture in the bottom row.

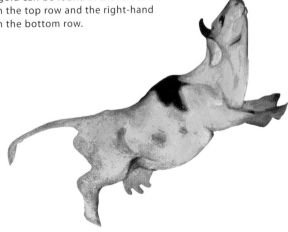

For Juliana and Sebastian

© Prestel Verlag, Munich · London · New York, 2011

© For the reproduced works by Marc Chagall and Wassily Kandinsky: VG Bild-Kunst, Bonn, 2011;
Pablo Picasso: Succession Picasso / VG Bild-Kunst, Bonn 2011;
Mark Rothko: Kate Rothko-Prizel & Christopher Rothko / VG Bild-Kunst, Bonn 2011

Prestel, a member of Verlagsgruppe Random House GmbH

Prestel Verlag, Munich

www.prestel.de

Prestel Publishing Ltd.
4 Bloomsbury Place
London WC1A 2QA

Prestel Publishing
900 Broadway, Suite 603
New York, NY 10003

www.prestel.com

Library of Congress Control Number is available; British Library Cataloguing-in-Publication Data: a catalogue record for this book is available from the British Library; Deutsche Nationalbibliothek holds a record of this publication in the Deutsche Nationalbibliografie;
detailed bibliographical data can be found under: http://dnb.ddb.de

Prestel books are available worldwide. Please contact your nearest bookseller or one of the above addresses for information concerning your local distributor.

Photo credits: If not otherwise stated, the original reproductions are from the archive of the publishing house. Artothek p. 12, 22, 23, 28, 32 – 3, 51, 53, 70; picture-alliance/dpa p. 34; Rheinisches Bildarchiv p. 56. Illustrations and drawing on pages 5, 8, 18 –19 bottom, 36, 49, 73, 89, 91, and photographs p. 11, 36 Silke Vry; color wheel p. 59: Sebastian Vry.

Translation: Cyntha Hall
Text editing: Brad Finger
Picture editing: Andrea Weißenbach
Design: Michael Schmölzl, agenten.und.freunde, Munich
Production: Natalie Senger
Lithography: reproline mediateam, Munich
Printing and binding: Neografia, Bratislava

MIX
Paper from responsible sources
FSC® C020353

Verlagsgruppe Random House FSC-DEU-0100
The FSC-certified paper Hello Fat Matt has been supplied by Deutsche Papier.

ISBN 978-3-7913-7053-8

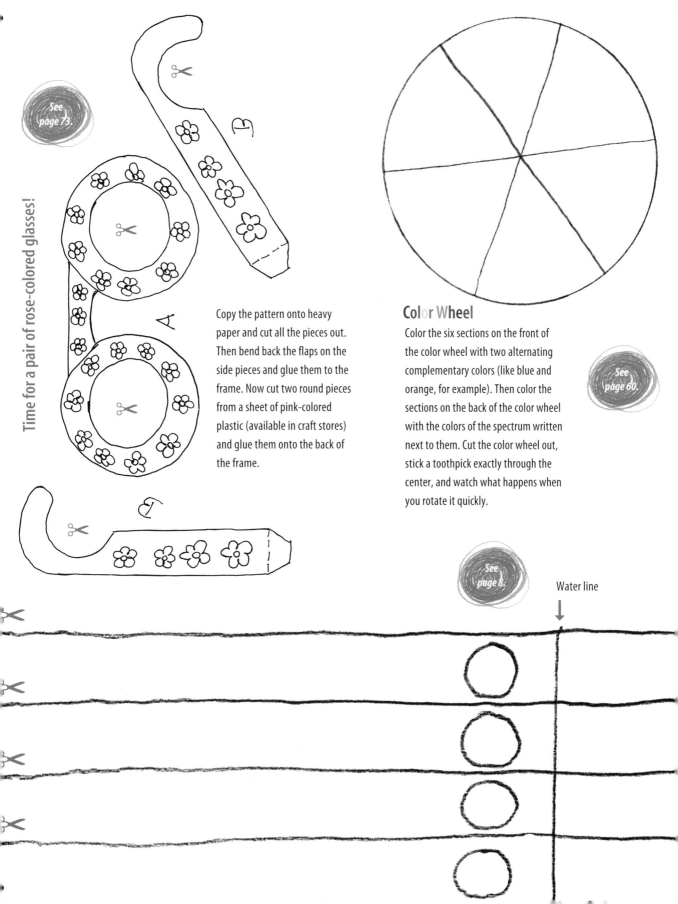

Time for a pair of rose-colored glasses!

See page 73.

B

A

B

Copy the pattern onto heavy paper and cut all the pieces out. Then bend back the flaps on the side pieces and glue them to the frame. Now cut two round pieces from a sheet of pink-colored plastic (available in craft stores) and glue them onto the back of the frame.

Color Wheel

Color the six sections on the front of the color wheel with two alternating complementary colors (like blue and orange, for example). Then color the sections on the back of the color wheel with the colors of the spectrum written next to them. Cut the color wheel out, stick a toothpick exactly through the center, and watch what happens when you rotate it quickly.

See page 60.

See page 8.

Water line

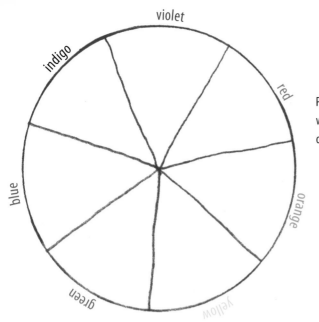

violet

indigo

red

blue

orange

green

yellow

Paint this side of the
wheel with the colors
of the spectrum!

Here you can give Venus a red wardrobe!

Color the clothing with pretty patterns in red and cut them out. If you like, you can glue Venus onto thin cardboard before you cut her out – so she'll be somewhat sturdier!

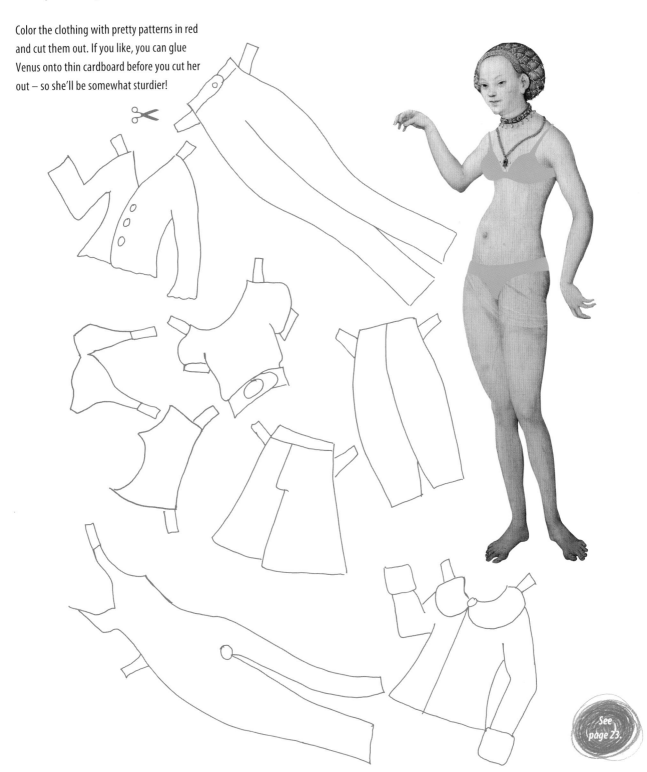

See page 23.

Your own stained-glass window

Cut out the pattern very carefully with a pair of pointed scissors. Glue colored pieces of tracing paper or tissue paper onto the back so that they cover over the holes. When you hold your finished picture up to the light, it will start to glow just like a stained-glass window.

See page 35.

How would Cézanne's picture look if it were painted with various cool, blue shades towards the bottom and warm, earthy colors towards the top? Try it out!

Make yourself a gold mask.

For this project, you'll need a sheet of gold foil from the craft store. Lay the gold paper on a slightly padded surface (a few layers of newspaper, for example). Then place the pattern shown here on the gold paper; mark the eyes, nose, and mouth with a pen; and cut holes to breathe and see through. Then round off the edges. ✂

Next, you can decorate the mask by pressing designs into the gold foil from behind with the pen.

Finally, poke two holes along the edges of the mask at about the height of your ears and attach a string or rubber band.

Franklin Pierce University

00194876